Miriam

WATCHES OVER BABY MOSES

Published in Nashville, Tennessee, by Tommy Nelson™,
a division of Thomas Nelson, Inc.
Managing Editor: Laura Minchew
Project Manager: Karen Gallini
Editor: Tama Fortner

Designed by Koechel Peterson & Associates
Digital color enhancement by Carolyn Guske
Cover illustration by Nathan Fowkes

"Deliver Us" and "River Lullaby." Words and music composed by
Stephen Schwartz © 1997 SKG Songs (ASCAP). Lyrics reprinted by permission.
International copyright secured. All rights reserved.

Library of Congress Cataloging-in-Publication Data

Simon, Mary Manz, 1948–
    Miriam watches over baby Moses : a story of faith and loyalty / by Mary Manz Simon.
      p.   cm. — (The Prince of Egypt values series)
    Summary: Miriam hides her baby brother, Moses, from the Pharaoh's soldiers
and remains loyal to her promise to protect him even in difficult times.
    ISBN 0-8499-5851-2
    1. Miriam (Biblical figure)—Juvenile literature. 2. Moses (Biblical leader)—
Juvenile literature. [1. Moses (Biblical leader) 2. Miriam (Biblical figure) 3. Bible
stories—O.T. 4. Loyalty.] I. Title. II. Series: Simon, Mary Manz, 1948– Prince of
Egypt values series.
BS580.M54S55   1998
222'.1209505—dc21
                                            98-38567
                                            CIP
                                            AC

Printed in the United States of America

98 99 00 01 02 03 QPH 9 8 7 6 5 4 3 2 1

THE PRINCE OF EGYPT

Miriam
WATCHES OVER BABY MOSES
A Story of Faith and Loyalty

by MARY MANZ SIMON

Timeless Values COLLECTION

Tommy NELSON

Thomas Nelson, Inc.
Nashville

*M*ud and sand, water and straw. Lift and pull, faster and faster! Day after day, the Hebrew slaves pounded out bricks to build temples and statues for Pharaoh, the king of Egypt. But even though the Hebrews were slaves, Pharaoh was afraid of them. He worried that because there were so many Hebrews, they might take over his country.

The number of Hebrews grew still larger and larger until one day, shaking with anger, Pharaoh ordered, "Every son who is born to the Hebrews shall be cast into the Nile River!" Then Pharaoh sent his soldiers into the streets to see that his order was carried out.

The Hebrew people cried out to God in despair. God had promised to deliver them one day from Egypt to the Promised Land. When would God keep that promise?

God heard the people's cry and remembered the promise. What the Hebrew people didn't know was that a young girl named Miriam— through her loyalty to her brother and her faith in God—would play an important role in keeping that promise. This is the story of Miriam's loyalty and faith.

From the time her brother was born, Miriam helped

her mother, Yocheved, hide him from Pharaoh's soldiers.

As they hid, Miriam often sang the baby a lullaby:

Brother, you're safe now and safe may you stay.

I'll love you and watch you, be with you each day.

Thirty days passed ... then forty days ... then fifty days. And still Miriam hid the baby. Her brother was growing bigger. It became harder to find a place to hide. Miriam grew more and more afraid that one of Pharaoh's soldiers would hear his gurgling baby talk or would see them racing from hiding place to hiding place.

So the family made a new plan. Yocheved used reeds from the Nile River to weave a special basket. She covered it all with pitch to make it waterproof. Then the family watched and waited.

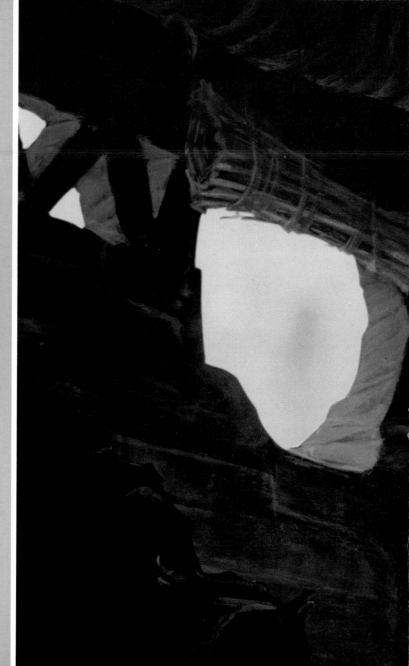

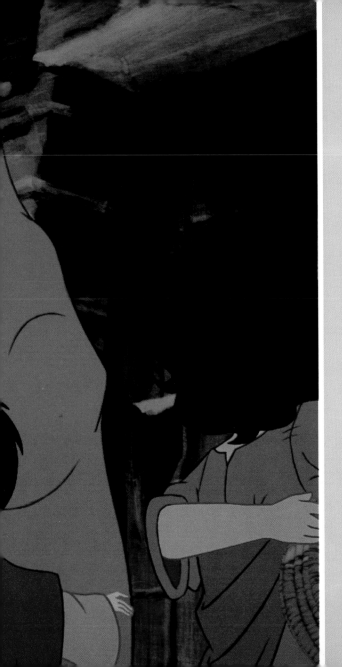

One day, when the baby was three months old, Pharaoh's soldiers thundered through the nearby streets, pounding on the doors of the Hebrews' huts and searching for baby boys. While Yocheved kept watch, Miriam held her brother and softly sang her promise to him:

Brother, you're safe now and safe may you stay.

I'll love you and watch you, be with you each day.

For a moment, the soldiers disappeared from the streets. Yocheved called to Miriam. It was time to use the basket. Miriam carried the tiny boat while her mother held the baby. They raced through the streets, down back alleys, and to the very edge of the Nile River.

The river was so big, and her brother was so small, Miriam wondered how he would ever survive. But she had faith that somehow God would keep her brother safe.

$\mathcal{M}$iriam watched her mother tenderly
place the baby in the basket and cover him
with the lid. As the basket slid into the waters
of the river, Yocheved sadly sang:

Hush now, my baby.

Be still love, don't cry.

Sleep as you're rocked by the stream.

Sleep and remember my last lullaby,

So I'll be with you when you dream.

River, O River,

Flow gently for me.

Such precious cargo you bear.

Do you know somewhere he can live free?

River, deliver him there.

Miriam was loyal. She would keep her promise to God: She would watch her brother. As the basket drifted farther and farther from the shore, Miriam followed it, peeping through the reeds and water plants.

The basket rocked as the waves lapped higher. Then the waves grew still rougher, and the basket bounced up and down. Water crashed against the sides. But the basket had been carefully and lovingly made. And so inside, the little boy stayed warm and dry.

$\mathcal{F}$inally the basket floated gently into the peaceful pools of the royal palace. Miriam crouched low, keeping her watch over the baby as one of the women reached out and opened the basket. With a cry of delight, the woman picked up the baby and held him close.

"This is one of the Hebrew children," she said, feeling sorry for the baby. And she named him Moses because he had been drawn out of the waters. Then she carried the baby into the palace.

As they disappeared from her sight, Miriam

sang a new lullaby:

> Brother, you're safe now and safe may
>
> you stay,
>
> For I have a prayer just for you . . .
>
> Grow baby brother, come back someday.
>
> Come and . . . deliver us . . . too.

And so, Moses became a prince of Egypt, while his sister was a slave. But Miriam remained loyal and kept her promise. She knew that Moses would one day remember her. And with great faith, she believed that just as she had been loyal to her brother, God would one day be loyal to her and to all the Hebrew people and deliver them from Egypt.

Although many years passed, God did indeed free the Hebrew slaves. And God used Moses, the tiny baby whose sister Miriam had so loyally watched over him, to deliver all the Hebrew people.

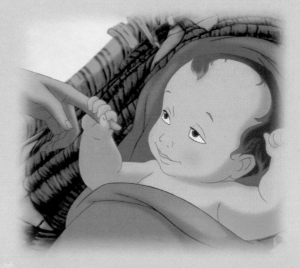

To Think About

Miriam was faithful to her brother, Moses. Her loyalty was tested many times—by the soldiers, by slavery, and even by the river. But she had made a promise, and she was determined to keep it.

Miriam was able to be loyal because she had faith in God. She trusted that God would somehow make a way to keep her brother safe. And God did just that.

There may be times when your loyalty is tested. For example, what would you do if a popular group of kids invited you to join them but didn't invite your best friend? You might be tempted to join the new group. But God wants you to treat your friend the way you would want to be treated. When you stick by your friend, everyone will see that you are a loyal person.

To Talk About

1. How did Miriam show that she was loyal to her brother?

2. When was a time you promised to be loyal?

3. What might have happened if Miriam hadn't kept her promise to watch over baby Moses?

4. Miriam was loyal, even when she faced danger. What makes it hard for you to be loyal?

5. Who has been loyal to you?

6. How do you choose to whom you should be loyal?

7. God promised to be with Miriam, and God promises to be with you. How do you feel about that?

8. How do you show loyalty and faithfulness to God?